UNVEILED

UNVEILED

IMAGES & INTIMATIONS OF MARRIAGE

Audrey Shehyn Vernick

HYPERION NEW YORK

Library of Congress Cataloging-in-Publication Data

Vernick, Audrey Shehyn.
   Unveiled : images and intimations of marriage / Audrey
Shehyn Vernick.—1st ed.
      p. cm.
   ISBN 0-7868-6828-7
   1. Weddings. 2. Weddings—Pictorial Works. 3. Marriage
customs and rites—United States—Pictorial works.
   4. Marriage customs and rites—United States. I. Title.

GT2690 .V47 2003
392.5—dc21
                                                    2002032717

Designed by Lorelle Graffeo

Hyperion books are available for special promotions and pre-
miums. For details contact Hyperion Special Markets, 77 West
66th Street, 11th floor, New York, New York 10023, or call
212-456-0133.

FIRST EDITION

10 9 8 7 6 5 4 3 2 1

FOR MY HUSBAND

FOREWORD

Every wedding has a story. The day unfolds full of excitement and trepidation, tension and love. Weddings are imbued with rich moments; they are complicated and enlivened by friends, family, anticipation, and anxiety. I have photographed dozens of weddings, acting as the official photographer, as a friend doing a favor, or simply as a guest unable to resist documenting this fascinating ritual. My role as photographer is to witness, investigate, and unveil the elusive truths surrounding the wedding-day dream.

The official wedding photographer's job is usually to encapsulate the ideal fantasy of the wedding in a single image: the blissful bride and groom in a loving embrace. Wedding portraits become cherished family heirlooms. One bride said to me, "I thought of all the wedding pictures I had seen over the years, and they were always so beautiful. I imagined myself in those same photos." I try to go beyond the typical posed portraits to create images that tell the real story of the day.

After years of photographing weddings and watching the subsequent marriages of friends, family, and clients, I have come to realize that a wedding is not the end, but the beginning. As a newlywed myself, I became deeply preoccupied with my thoughts on marriage. I wanted to discover what it meant to other people, and what it means to me. I very much wanted to know *why* we marry. Is marriage still an important part of our social fabric in a divorce-prone society? What is the significance of the ceremony in a culture devoid of rituals, where weddings have become a commercial phenomenon? I turned to my current and former subjects for answers.

I tried to interpret these larger questions by asking the couples more specific ones, such as: Were you looking to get married? Do you view marriage as a lifelong commitment? What roles did tradition and religion play in your wedding? What was the highlight of your wedding day? Does marriage make you a better person? I encouraged couples to consider how ritual and expectation had dictated their "choices." As the subjects of this book recounted their thoughts, wishes, and needs, my project became an effort to deconstruct the meaning of marriage and the ceremony that joins two people together. Some people talked about their fears of coming from divorced families, even though they expected *their* relationships to be different. Gay couples reminded me that there are still certain people in this country who cannot legally get married in the eyes of the state. Others described the unexpected, unmitigated joy they felt on their wedding days, and their hopes for lasting marriages.

I worked with a diverse group of interviewees. Some of the couples I spoke with had been married a few weeks, others more than a decade. They ranged in age from twenty to sixty-something; they were straight and gay, poor and wealthy, compatible and seemingly incompatible, and of different religious backgrounds. I witnessed a broad range of weddings, from the backyard barbecue to the luxury hotel.

There were certain undercurrents that existed from couple to couple, regardless of their more specific circumstances. One was the desire of each couple to create a ceremony that was indicative of the uniqueness of their relationship. They all wanted to have a nontraditional wedding; they hoped their wedding would be a reflection of themselves and say something about their particular story. Yet weddings are always traditional, by their very definition. We all have ideas about what a wedding looks like, how it is *supposed* to be done. Most couples walk down an aisle and exchange vows, most have family and friends present, most have cake and dancing. We accept the conventional structure of a wedding even though the details may vary considerably. Many couples told me, "I don't know why we did it this way. It's just the way you do a wedding." Perhaps traditions are a way to calm the tension, to distract us from the monumental step we are about to take.

After interviewing nearly one hundred brides and grooms, I began to understand more fully that rituals are a way to connect to something bigger than yourself. Ceremony is a way of distinguishing the sacred from the mundane—a way of elevating the ordinary and celebrating changes in life that would otherwise go unnoticed. A wedding symbolizes the advent of a new way of living.

What became clear in the interviews was that we don't often think about what marriage really means to us. When I asked people for their definitions of marriage, nearly everyone—even those who had been married for years—said, "You know, I have never really thought about that." We have assumptions and preconceptions, but few of us have a clear idea about the actual meaning of marriage.

So why do we get married? For some, there is a sense of security when your partner makes a public commitment to you. The community sees your relationship as indisputable. The official bond is stronger, too, as your legal standing changes. The couples I interviewed gave myriad reasons: We marry to make ourselves happy, to have intimacy, to start a family. We marry because we have been living together for too long and people keep asking when we're going to take the leap. We marry so we won't be lonely anymore, or because we have always had a fantasy that involved a white dress, lots of flowers, and a groom. We marry because, well, why not? We marry as an expression of the deep love we feel for another human being. We marry because our parents had a great marriage, or because our parents had a terrible marriage but we are going to do it better, different, right. We marry to satisfy our longing for someone who will complement our personalities and make our lives feel more complete.

I have spent the past two years examining the changing nature and changing perceptions of marriage, exploring what it means for two people to declare their love in front of their families and friends, God or the state. As a result of my investigations, my opinions about marriage have not changed as much as they have been expanded. I believe in marriage more, because I now understand that inside marriage vulnerability is allowed—embraced, even—and fear of exposure is relieved by trust. Marriage can be a place to let down your mask, to be yourself in a culture where so much is expected. It is a way to define your roles, to say, "This is who I am." Marriage remains the ultimate goal for most people because it is where one's deepest self is unveiled. As one bride told me, "Marriage is a challenge. But it's the most exciting and romantic challenge you can dive into."

UNVEILED

SARAH

I was very calm when I got dressed. I was thinking, "Do I have the right makeup? Am I going to be pretty enough?" You start the day in your slip, with a clean face, and you have to build it all: put on the makeup, put on the underskirt, put on the dress, put on the flowers, put on the perfume, something blue, something old, and you just hope that the sum of all that is greater than the parts.

The second that I started walking toward the altar I totally lost it; I burst into tears. I had not prepared myself mentally for what was going to happen. I am such a sap; all of the emotion came out. It is deep stuff, the ritual of marriage. You really *are* leaving one family and creating another. I was surprised by how scary and powerful it felt. I spent the ceremony weeping, worrying about my mascara, and loving it.

I was undone by how moving our wedding was, and how buoyed up by love I felt. There was so much love. I was feeling so high and everyone seemed to rise up to it. People said insightful and supportive things about me. I felt celebrated, like I was *seen* for who I really am. When everybody came together, they all agreed that I was a good person—they all loved me. That was so healing. It was my fifteen minutes. I was truly filled with joy, and so excited that we were going to run off and start our life together.

My wedding surpassed all of my expectations. You think about all the planning and the expense and the drama—how could anything be worth that? Like spending $2,000 on a wedding dress that you'll never wear again, spending this much on the cake, the chairs, the caterer, the band. The actual day was so profound that it was not only worthwhile to go through all that, it surpassed all those things.

SONNY

I didn't want to get married until I thought I wasn't going to be able to score any more dates. I didn't expect to get married until I was old. But I had never met anyone like Mharla twenty-four years into my life; I thought it could be another twenty-four years until I met anybody like her again, and there is just so much time. My life would have only half as much potential without Mharla, and when I recognized that I just knew. The most powerful thing in our relationship is our relationship with God. Mharla was a blessing sent to me from God, and when you have a gift from God you don't want to take advantage of it, you want to keep it as pure as possible.

Once we got married—that was the official green light to go ahead with our life. We are a family now—me, her, and her baby, together. They are mine. We have been the perfect complement to one another. I cannot imagine my life any other way. I feel at peace. I look forward to spending the rest of my life with Mharla.

JANE

After my last relationship ended I lost hope. I thought, "That's it. It will be me and my twenty-three cats in my studio, until I die." I was open to meeting people, but I didn't have any expectations. I wondered, "How many more dead-end relationships do I need to be in before I find my life partner? When is it just going to be right?"

My girlfriends and I had put together this list of qualities that I was looking for in the "perfect" man. At that point in life, I knew what I was looking for, and I knew what I didn't want. Even though it seems like a ridiculous thing to do and we were very silly about it, in a way it made me realize that I *did* know what I was looking for. In another way, I worried, "Well, I'm never going to find *this*. This man does not exist."

Then I met George. We took it very slow at first. We made sure this was a conscious choice that both of us were making together, rather than quickly falling into something before we had emotions for the other person. Our communication was clear from the beginning; we were open and honest with each other. There were no games, none of that dishonesty or weirdness. And it turned out George had most of the qualities on my list.

We talked about getting married a couple of months after we met. It was fast but it was so apparent. Everything clicked. I had never been more clear about a decision in my entire life. We had a deep understanding of each other without having to work at it. He made me swoon, and I had not felt that way in a long time.

The wedding took a lot of planning. I thought, "This is a lot to deal with. Maybe we should just elope." At first, I didn't think other people needed to be there. It is a commitment between us. Then I realized it is also about two families coming together. It is about having your friends around to support you. I decided that I wanted everyone to be there.

I got a lot of advice—people needed to tell us how to do things. "You're not having a cake? Oh." And, "You're not wearing white? Oh." I was doing it differently because I was not comfortable with what those traditions meant. I wanted to take bits of existing traditions and make them new and meaningful for us. We walked down the aisle together, and my mom said, "You can't walk down the aisle with him! You are not married!" I said, "George and I are partners, and we are walking into this together as partners, but thanks for your suggestion." I learned to say that a lot—"Thanks for your suggestion."

I wanted to wear a red dress. I didn't like what the white dress is supposed to mean. Initially, that tradition meant that a woman was virginal, totally pure, and thank God because that is how the men want them. I didn't want a princess ballgown. It's just not who I am. I never wear white—everyone thought I was going to wear black. I wanted something that was *me*.

I think that institutionalized weddings have so much inherent sexism, they seem so formal and devoid of real emotions. We wanted to create something new. The ceremony was totally meaningful to us—it was a serious commitment. We wanted a big bash. We wanted endless streams of champagne, bountiful fun. Our wedding represented us. I can look at it and say it was a real George-and-Jane day from beginning to end.

JOHN

I was thinking, "I can't believe that I'm about to go through with this. I'm actually going to go out there and tell everyone, 'You have to consider us husbands now.'" I was nervous and apprehensive, although I knew I wanted to do it; I knew I wanted to be married. I was surprised at how easy it was. I thought that I wouldn't know what to say, but it all sort of gushed out of me.

Marriage is a declaration that some person you are not related to is closer to you in every respect than any of your blood relatives. It rivals the strength of the parental bond. As life goes on, it eclipses all of your blood relationships.

When you are gay, there is no pressure to get married. You have to really work at it. There are some people who cannot quite grasp the concept of two guys getting married. Or they assume you can get married and it's all legal, just like straight people. They don't understand that gay marriage has absolutely no legal standing. I had only come out to my family when I started dating Mark. I wanted to make it clear to everyone that this was a lifelong relationship. That is what marriage is about—getting society to acknowledge a change in your relationship from two guys shacking up to two guys who are in love and who will be together for the rest of their lives.

ASHA

I have a love marriage. My sisters had arranged marriages—all of them except me. My brother's marriage was arranged in India. In our culture it is just understood that you are going to have an arranged marriage.

I met Rakesh when I was sixteen. Our parents tried their best to stop our relationship. I was so young and I was already talking to boys. When I told my dad that I wanted to marry Rakesh, he was in shock. He said, "You don't know what love is about until you are older." Eventually, he said, "In order for this to happen, you have to finish college and wait until you are twenty-three." He thought that I should be able to stand on my own two feet. He was worried that I would throw my education away for love. I had to prove to him that I was not dumb enough to do that.

I set my priorities straight and finished college in three years, and we asked our parents again. My dad finally approved. All we wanted was to say "I do" in front of everybody so they knew that we were a couple, and go on with our lives. We knew we were not going to get married unless we had blessings from both sides, even if it took ten years. We were not willing to break up over it, but we were also not willing to elope. We just could not do that to our families.

In arranged marriages, the parents are not looking so much for the perfect match for the guy—they are looking for a bride who is going to take care of the family and run the household. When I was growing up I thought, "When I get married, I am going to have to be a servant." But Rakesh is not like that. A lot of Indian marriages are not based on friendship. You get to date for about a month, but you are basically set to get married. Your friendship does not grow until you have been married for a long time. I got to be his friend first, which is what I cherish the most. The friendship is the best part.

I have my own goals in life. I told him from the beginning, "I'm not going to be your typical Indian wife who stays at home. I got educated for a reason—I'm going to work." I am still getting educated: I am working on my master's degree. Rakesh is very supportive of that. We both know that we are not going to live a life where the wife runs a motel while the husband goes out and plays. It's going to be different for us.

"I kept running and getting things. I wanted coffee, so I jumped up to get it.

The fella doing my makeup kept saying, 'You're princess for the day.

Somebody else will get it for you!' But everybody else was busy. I said,

'I guess I don't make a very good princess,' and walked off to get my coffee."

—PEGGY

LISELI

I'm not a frilly, fluffy person. I don't like makeup but that didn't matter. I had to wear it. Everybody was saying, "You have to—it's your wedding day." They thought it was really funny that they got to make me up. They kept saying, "Ha ha, you have to sit there and take it." At one point the room was full of comments like, "Have you sparkled? Can I fluff you? Have you been puffed?" My best friend from college has always been the girlie one. She was like, "Come on Liseli, just a little lipstick." It was fun for her. The girls just got to hang out. It was like a reunion. We all had a connection. It was just nice to have this group of women around, and having my mom there. My mom was having little hissy fits, and that's a good thing. It made everything seem normal.

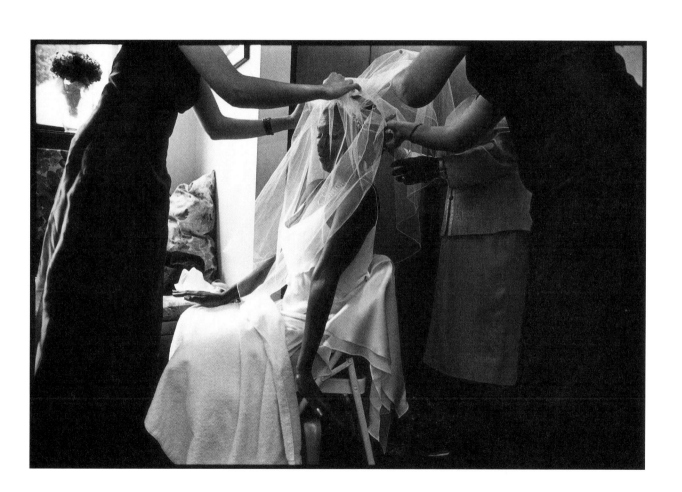

JOHN M.

Our wedding was fantastic. It was the most wonderful wedding I have ever been to. The best part was when Pattie talked about how she was able to be disappointed in me, which was a boon to her because in past relationships she had repressed her disappointments, which meant that she couldn't really feel for herself. I thought that was just spectacular. Never heard that in a wedding—never. Nobody had. You don't usually say anything negative; you say something big and marital about how you know you are going to have good times. But that's abstract; it doesn't get down to the nitty-gritty. When we complain that we hate each other, and we get furious at each other, and annoyed and walled off, then real things happen. Well, the service got closer to that. I loved that about it.

Some people had trouble with what Pattie said, but others understood. I will never forget when I told another couple about it at a party some time later—they obviously weren't getting along in their marriage. The woman got it right away. "Boy, I wish he was like that," she said. And her husband said, "Why would you want her to complain?" Because, well, then you know how she feels.

To me, the meaning of life is to find out about yourself, and the most efficacious way of doing that is to be in a relationship. In relationships you get at the things that you want to protect; you can't hide from hurt or anger, or avoid things that are too upsetting. I want to have those feelings. I think the secret to a marriage's survival is understanding that complaints, all sorts of "negative" expressions, are garbled, distorted, desperate attempts to say something meaningful. If you figure out what the hidden meaning is of these things that just drive you nuts, then that's the secret. It's not something that you should try to get rid of or ignore.

We have these ordinary experiences that everyone has—joys and sorrows and anger and fights and hurts—all those things go on with everybody. If you can stand back and talk about your relationship, look at it as you might view characters in a movie, then you have all sorts of feelings that you otherwise wouldn't acknowledge. You can have empathy for that other couple, and appreciate their successes and joys. You have a relationship *about* the relationship and that one is more fulfilling than the actual relationship, in some ways. There is a deeper kind of love that you get from really seeing your plight in relation to that other person.

LISA

The morning of the wedding was so tense. Things were not going well. I was so nervous—I was a robot. All I could think was, "We have to do this, then we have to do that, and then we'll do that." The only emotion was stress, that was all I was feeling. I do remember having this aside thought of, "Holy shit, this is really happening!"

For months leading up to the wedding I had this bizarre neurosis that something was going to go wrong and the wedding would not happen. I was convinced that something completely out of my control was going to intervene. I would wake up at night with my heart pounding. I was not anxious about anything in particular. I was not going to sleep thinking, "The invitations aren't done!" It was just general anxiety that would hit me in the middle of the night.

On the wedding day what struck me was that it actually happened. No plane went down, no major tornado came through and ripped up the church. I thought, "We're here. Oh my God, we're here. I cannot believe that this is really happening."

After we were married I felt relieved. I felt like we could start our lives. It seemed that everything had been on hold except for the wedding. Once the wedding was over we could be together, living together. We could go back to a normal life.

We never expected the wedding to change our lives significantly. Marriage was just another logical step in the evolution of our relationship. People get freaked out about getting married, like it is going to change your life, big time. I never saw it that way. We had already lived together, and I knew everything about him. I felt as if I couldn't get any more devoted to this person; I could not possibly love him any more.

There are probably more practical reasons than emotional ones to have a wedding. For me, it didn't matter either way, so why not go ahead and do it? It seemed like a logical progression. I guess we are just traditional. This is the course of one's life. You could come up with a million reasons not to get married, but if you feel like you have found the right person, then what's stopping you?

MHARLA

I had never dated outside my race before. I used to have issues about interracial relationships—I thought that the races should just stick together. Sonny was falling in love with me and I was falling in love with him, but I had an issue that he was Mexican. A few months after we started dating I told him how I felt, and his heart was broken. It made me feel so bad. I didn't realize it would hurt him like that. From that point on, I no longer had an issue. I was ready to move forward. All of that just went away after I saw how hurt he was. I realized that could not be a reason to keep us apart. Love has no limits or boundaries, and it is certainly not limited to racial backgrounds. God put us together and God chose someone for me who was outside my race.

GINA

I had always wanted to get married. I imagined wearing the big fancy dress and all that little-girl stuff. I thought, "This is how people have weddings." Now it surprises me that I didn't question things more, that I didn't say, "Why is it done that way? Why can't we do it another way?"

You can get caught up in all the details and the planning. You have your "to do" list, all these things you *have* to do. It is important to remind yourself along the way, "Why are we doing this?" At one point Hobie took me out of town for a long weekend. He said, "Put the *Martha Stewart Living* down. You are out of control." I was trying to do everything and I was getting carried away.

Once we were married I felt a little let down, actually. I didn't have any second thoughts, but it became clear how big a step it was. You can't understand the commitment when you are caught up in the romance of it. Our meeting felt like a real fairy tale. I was whisked off my feet and there was this flurry of activity. When we got through the excitement of being engaged, getting married, being newlyweds, and got into living together day to day, that was difficult. Then we were doing laundry together. The fairy tale was over. It isn't that we fell into a mundane life, but it did feel abrupt. I had to adjust to the fact that the butterfly feeling in my stomach wasn't going to last until our fiftieth anniversary.

Now that we have been married for five years, I see that it is so much more than that fairy tale. You reach a whole other level with that person. I feel like we have created our own family out here on our own. This is my family. I knew I wanted something different from what my parents had, and I have gotten that. I feel fortunate. I get to be married to my best friend.

JP

The absolute best thing about marriage, truly, is sitting around with my wife, my son, and the dog, with nothing to do. All of us get into bed together—sometimes it drives Amy nuts because there isn't any room and everybody is squirming. It opens my heart wide to have us all just hanging out. The dog is looking for a tennis ball in the bed, the kid is running around in his underwear, jumping up and down, and Amy is complaining that she doesn't have enough room. There is nothing that goes on, nothing that happens. It is the most important place in the world—a place to touch base, to say we can all fit in the same spot and get along.

I feel a real awareness of the awesome responsibility of being married. I do not take it lightly. I take the importance of Amy's happiness as equal to my own. The most important thing is for us to work everything out, no matter what. I may not get the chance to do everything in my life that I want because there is one goal that I have that is higher, and that is to have a lasting, fulfilling marriage.

DANIEL

I looked at other people getting married, and they had this "till death do us part" attitude. I thought, "Well, do they really feel that way?" This culture we live in, it's more about "till unhappiness do us part." Everyone is chasing after happiness and then as soon as they are not happy, they are done. When Tanis and I were getting married, I don't think that we ever said to each other, "You are the one for the rest of my life." We said, "I hope this works out." I always wonder if we took too light of an approach, if we should have been more serious.

There were things that we loved about each other, but there was a variety of ways in which we were so very different. It was truly an "opposites attract" situation. Being married made it more serious—we were more devoted to each other. If we had just lived together I don't think that we would have been as committed to working things out. There were moments when I would reflect, "Well, what if we were in this situation and we weren't married?" I had a definite answer for that. We would have split. Actually, we would have never gotten married.

Getting married was a very big step for me. I was conscious of the life-changing part of it. I thought, "Is this something I am capable of?" That was weighing on me. The first few years of our marriage were difficult. The wedding is only one part of it—it's a ceremony. So many people get swept up into "the wedding," and what this wedding is going to do. But the wedding isn't going to do what you think it is going to do for a marriage; you can't be fooled into that. There is more to a marriage. That is when the real work starts.

PETER

There is a societal expectation to get married. The older you get, the harder it becomes. I was forty-five. I told a friend the week before I met Connie that I didn't think I would ever get married.

When we first met, I came away knowing that something had happened. I didn't even know how to call her up and ask her out. I was afraid she would say no. I wanted to marry her, I knew that, even though I had not gone out with her yet. I did not know how to get from A to B, or, for me, it would look more like from A to Z. On our second date we went on a walk together. I said, "By the way, Connie, you might just be interested in a walk, but actually I want to marry you." I never had any second thoughts.

My wedding was completely different than I expected. I did not expect to find somebody, and I did not expect to get married outside. I never met anybody who had their guests walk a mile to get to the wedding. I knew walking would calm me down, so I wanted us all to take a walk. People were coming from all over the country—it was a way for people to meet one another along the way. There were some wet spots on the trail, and I was concerned about how people were going to get over them. People did get their feet muddy. It is not often you go to a wedding that has an obstacle course.

Marriage is a celebration. I was starting a new life with Connie. I felt committed to her long before we got married, but I was wearing a wedding ring that I had never worn before. It is more of a public statement. The marriage is not just between Connie and me. I need the support of other people around me.

I don't think marriage is hard. Am I one hundred percent happy every day? No, of course not. It's life, there are two of you. But if I had the opportunity to marry Connie again, I would. You learn more in the difficult times when you put them into perspective. It's a new adventure, a rite of passage. It's like walking through a door—you will never be the same.

ADRIA

I remember standing at the back of the church and taking my dad's arm. He was all choked up. It was a big moment. I saw the look on his face; he wasn't smiling. He looked like he was trying to hold back tears. Luckily, I had a veil over my face so people could not see me, because I was crying, too. When those doors opened and I saw everybody—my family and friends, people I hadn't seen in years—that was an incredible moment.

My ideas of marriage come from my parents. They have been married thirty-four years and they are still in love with each other. That is the model I grew up with. I feel as strongly about our marriage as I do about my parents' marriage. So much of what is important in our relationship is based on what I learned from them. Work is important, and so are friends, but family is what really matters.

Brian and I are different religions, we are from different cultures, but we see that as something positive. It may be more work at times trying to understand where the other person is coming from, or some custom that they have, but it is rewarding. Brian is not just my husband, he is also my best friend, the person I intend to raise my children with, the person I want to grow old with. Marriage is one of the best things I have done. It is also one of the hardest things I have done. It is a big commitment.

SUSAN

We put hours and hours into picking flowers and dresses, but it was the time that we spent together thinking about our vows and our ceremony that made the difference for us. We sat down and talked about what it meant to us to get married. I don't remember my exact words, but they just flowed. They came out of me, and I didn't edit them. It was so real. I didn't worry about the fact that a hundred people were going to hear me say these things. It was what I needed to say. You can bring so much of yourself to the ceremony. Some people think it's a formality—that you should just get it over with as quickly as possible. But it's that formality that ties you together.

The most meaningful part of our wedding was the bedeken before the actual ceremony. Our rabbi had everybody get into a circle and give us their blessings—the wedding party and our closest friends and family. There was an incredible sense of warmth and support. I could see my mother's face, my friends' faces. We were getting personal expressions from each individual. It was intimate. There was nothing rehearsed about it.

Our wedding was sophisticated and classy. Barefoot on the beach is definitely not our style. We have a videotape of our wedding, but we haven't looked at it yet. In my mind it was just so perfect. It was exactly how I wanted it. I feel like if I watch the videotape I'll be critical, and I'll say I didn't do this right, I didn't do that right. I don't know if I'll ever watch that videotape.

JESUS

I was nervous because of the way I was dressed. It was different. I thought, "I don't wear this every day. Imagine, this is a special day." You put on the suit and then take it off, but the memories remain. From the moment I put it on, I thought that was the day I was going to change, that was the day the devil would come out of me. After being naughty in my first marriage, I knew that was over. My evil ways ended there. People were not happy about our wedding. I knew some people were talking about me. I was still married when I met Bertha. At first she didn't want to get married—she had never been married and didn't want to be. But we had a child together. Then I was able to convince her.

I was married in the same place for my first marriage. That one was simpler; this one was with a nice dress and flowers and all that. Everything was different from the time it started. This time, all my friends were there. There were more than three hundred people. Some friends weren't even able to get in. We didn't have much money, but we did it simply and happily. I made all the food. So many people helped us. I'm very happy with the way we did the wedding. Everything came out as I hoped it would, thanks to God.

ALICE

In Vietnamese culture a wedding has to be done correctly. You can't pick and choose the traditions you want to follow, you have to do it all. That's what our families wanted and we wanted to respect that. You can't just drive to city hall and sign a paper and be married. It is not just between De and me. We wanted Buddha to accept us and take us in as a family, to protect us and guide us to do the right thing. We wanted to have his blessing for a long, happy marriage.

In our culture, when a woman marries she belongs to the man's family. At our wedding, my mom said, "As De's wife, you are still my daughter, but part of you is now his family's daughter. You have to follow, accept, and support your husband and his family. Treat everyone in that family as your own." In the old days a bride would move away to a different village and her family might be sad because they were losing a daughter. But times change. My mom seemed happy that I had someone to take care of me, rather than worrying about losing me. I know that I will be a good wife and a good daughter-in-law.

This marriage is for life. I failed in my first marriage. I was young and I had no idea that when you commit to each other there are certain things you have to give up, certain things you have to sacrifice. It never crossed my mind that I would get married again. But De is the one I want to spend my life with. We are going to hold on to each other no matter what happens. He is my whole world now.

RICH

Men have this naive impression that marriage changes your life for the worse. Growing up, we always had these jokes that maybe we would just get a dog and a ski cabin and live like bachelors. When you are twenty-three, sitting around with a bunch of guys watching football and drinking beer, that is the impression of marriage that you give one another: Life—or the aspects of it that you particularly enjoy—will end. All of a sudden you are going to be watching videos and living in the suburbs. As I got older, I was able to see tangibly that my close friends, likely the same ones I was sitting around having that conversation with ten years earlier, were married and genuinely happy. That made me feel better. It made me feel more comfortable with my decision.

Relationships are a part of a continuum. If you think about a wedding as a pivotal event—the typical bachelor's fear that your lifestyle will forever change—it is harder to adjust. We are comfortable with our marriage because it feels like the continuation of a journey that we are taking together. It's a question of whether you let those moments define you, or whether you take what you want from them and make them yours.

CRAIG

It was love at first sight. I was enthralled. I knew I wanted to be with her and I would do whatever it took.

After we had been together for two or three months, I presented a ring to Gabriella. I didn't have a lot of money so I bought the only ring I could. I wanted us to be together, there was no doubt in my mind. Our parents said, "Oh, no. You shouldn't do this. It's too soon." That burst the bubble. So we thought, "Okay, let's just calm ourselves now." It was years later that we truly took the dive.

I was content to just be with her, but after a while getting married became important for Gabriella. We had been living together for a few years, and her parents were always saying, "When are you going to get married?" Marriage was not particularly important to me at that point; I just knew that I wanted to be with her.

It was Gabriella's thirtieth birthday. I asked her what she wanted and she said, "A ring." I didn't think *engagement* ring. It went straight over my head. My mum was visiting from England so we went out shopping. I found this nice little ring and my mum mentioned, "Are you sure that is what she wants? She meant a *ring*." I thought, "Oh, God!" We went home and Gabriella said she would like me to take a look at this ring that she found. I went to the shop and asked the jeweler if Gabriella had been there. He said, "yes," and showed me what she had been looking at. He pointed to the ring and it said wedding all over it. It was screaming, "Marry me!"

All of a sudden what had started out as just a ring for a birthday had become a *wedding* ring. I had to sit down. My mum said, "What are you going to do? Are you going to marry her? Do you love her? Do you want to be with her for the rest of your life?" I just looked at her, she looked back, and there was silence, staring at the walls. I said, "Yeah, I do," and I went back and bought the ring.

Gabriella's birthday came and she got lots of things, but no ring. That year we went traveling quite a bit. That ring stayed with me for eight months. It was stuffed in my sock in the bottom of a rucksack, waiting for the right time to give it to her. That ring has traveled the world. We went to Costa Rica, Guatemala, Britain. We were in Kauai, and again the ring was with me. I managed to gather enough strength and will to actually go through with it. I brought out the ring and said, "Gabriella, there is something I would like to ask you. Will you marry me?" She said, "Oh, yes!" She was so happy. Then she opened the box and said, "Oh my God! It is *the* ring!"

Marriage is public, but the vows are deeply personal. It is a promise. I have said to Gabriella many times that we would still be together had we not been married. The commitment that I have to Gabriella is absolute.

NUME

Julie wasn't into having the Thai wedding with all the different ceremonies. She wanted it to be short and not include a whole weekend of events. But I didn't want to do the quick thing in Vegas or Reno. I figured you only get married once. I wanted to include our families, our cultures, our religions. That is who we are, it is part of us. My parents are very religious; I was paying tribute to them by having a Thai wedding. I wanted Buddha to witness and be a part of our marriage. I wanted all of the traditions: being married in a Thai temple, being married in the Chinese tradition at her family's house, lighting the incense and having the monks present. I wanted both cultures to unite us coming together. Marriage is a big deal. I didn't want to just get it over with, like going through a fast-food restaurant drive-through. I wanted the whole package. I wanted our ceremony to be something that I would always remember.

PATTIE

Falling in love wasn't falling. It was slow. Actually, it's still happening. It's not like you fall in love and then it ends. You keep finding out more about the person. It's amazing, when you find the right person, that it keeps happening after all that time.

We had talked about marriage but we were in our forties. You tend to collect things as you get older, and we both had children from our first marriages. We didn't want to have to deal with all that distributing, and the prenuptial, and then talking about a will. What made us get married was that we wanted to adopt a child. Somebody at the agency said it would be better for us if we were married. It was another thing that pushed us over the edge. We put our wedding together in two weeks, which was great because we couldn't get all anal about the planning. It doesn't sound very romantic. I always felt like all three of us were married—me, John, and the baby.

When you are young, you are idealistic. You don't think about the things that are going to make you sad, or that anything will ever go wrong. When you get married, you make all these promises but you don't think about the negativity. You don't think about infertility or illness or death or tragedy. Those things do happen, though. The second half of your life, that's what it's about—facing your parents getting ill, disappointments you have in your own body, financial limitations. We knew that would happen, we knew that there would be times in our lives when we could not cope. That is a big thing between us, to have a realistic idea of what our life will be like together. I would say that we are not very romantic.

Getting married is like getting a facelift, it takes a lot of worry off of you. You have someone you can count on. There is a safety net underneath you, that's how I envision it. But you could still fall through at any moment. That's how marriage is: You count on it in a way, but then you never know what is going to happen. You can never take your partner for granted. That person defines you and makes you the best and the worst that you could possibly be. Inside your marriage is where you share your most important, intimate self.

"Show up on time, keep your damn mouth shut,

and if she says smile, you smile."

— J P

GARRY

My proposal stands out as one of those singular moments that I will always remember. When I dropped to one knee, held out the little box, and asked him to marry me, I knew that I was doing exactly the right thing, not just for myself, but for him, too. It just felt *right*.

We live in a society of disposable relationships. There are certain traditions that take place in our culture that allow us to separate those relationships from the committed ones. A wedding is one of those traditions. A lot of our gay friends don't understand—they see marriage as a heterosexual convention. They don't see how it is relevant within the gay community. But I think it is important that you establish a point of distinction between just dating someone versus having a commitment to a life partner—and that this distinction is made to yourselves, your community, and your family. The wedding symbolized that transition. It turned out to be a perfect way to do it because it was clearly understood by everyone. Our marriage is absolutely a life-long proposition. I distinguish it from any relationship that I have been in for that reason.

Everybody has been to a million heterosexual weddings—people know what to expect. But our guests had no idea what they were walking into. We were empowered by our rabbi to choose aspects of the Jewish tradition that would mean something to us. We were married under Eric's grandfather's tallis and the kiddush cup that held the wine was my grandparents'. We integrated our own traditions and our Judaic heritage into a ceremony that was distinctly Jewish. That meant a lot to us because we both live active lives as Jews.

The wedding was the launching of a new direction. We were saying, "This is a new course for us."

In Judaism, the apex of that is the ketubah, the signing of the contract between two parties, acknowledging that they want to spend their lives together. The top of our ketubah says: "I have found the one in whom my soul delights." That is a very appropriate thing because I *have* found the one in whom my soul delights.

For me, one of the best moments in our wedding was reading what I had written for Eric. Normally, we don't share those thoughts with other people. We may be intimate by holding hands, or sharing a kiss, but to actually express how we feel is something entirely different. That was my chance to say it all.

RAKESH

We knew we were going to have a traditional Indian wedding, although our wedding was really different from what they do in my caste. I didn't understand anything in the ceremony, I was just going along with what the priest said. It's not what I wanted to do, it's what they wanted me to do. I was worried. I thought, "What if I do something wrong?" I had to hold a coconut in my hand, and they believe if you drop it, it's bad luck. Everyone was staring at me. Those things were nerve-wracking. The moment when I put the mangalsutra on Asha's neck is like exchanging the rings in American weddings. That was the only thing I understood because we also do that in our caste. That was the most important to me because our parents also wear the mangalsutra.

As far as tradition goes, I don't expect her to be at home taking care of me. I tell her, "If you don't want to cook, don't cook. Either we will go out or I will make grilled cheese." We were born and raised in America, we know we both have to work to get somewhere in life.

SKIP

Our wedding was great, but it was over just like that. I wish somebody had told me how depressing the next day is. It is the blackest depression. There is a big emotional build-up—you have all of your best friends and your family there and all of this stuff is going on—then all of a sudden it is just completely over. We were shell-shocked. I cried, which is rare for me. I felt empty and drained. It had nothing to do with being married; it was not at all about "now I am married and this is the rest of my life" depression. It is clear to me now why people leave for their honeymoons right away. It would have been nice to just wake up in Bali.

JENNIFER

I was five and a half months pregnant when we got married. David always says that we had been going in that direction and we probably would have gotten married anyway. I think that's true, but who knows how long we would have gone along if I hadn't gotten pregnant. It certainly was a big impetus. It brought up a bit of shame about being pregnant and getting married. We are so inculcated with this idea of how it *should* be. I wanted to plan the wedding for sooner rather than later so I wouldn't be extremely pregnant. In retrospect, I'm glad that in the photos you can see that I'm pregnant. That the baby was part of the ceremony created even more joy, so in its own way it was perfect.

When I think about our wedding day, I am filled with joy and ecstasy. It felt like a sacred process. We were sealing our commitment to one another to walk down this path together and see what unfolds. It was very powerful. It felt mystical in many ways. I remember standing under the huppah and the rabbi blessing us—I just wanted the ceremony to go on and on and on. It was ecstatic. I felt so connected to David, so proud and content. I was feeling love from all the people who were there to participate and witness. There was a rush of emotions from what had just transpired. After the ceremony I had a sense of being unbelievably happy to have a partner, and we had this baby coming. My wishes had been fulfilled—I was getting what I wanted.

DANA

Marriage is not the ideal fantasy that we pretend it is. I have lived through some things and I know what it is about. I learned a lot from my first marriage. I am older now, wiser. I know that I will not be with anyone whom I don't trust. I also learned that men are a different species, period. They are totally different. You cannot change them. What you see is what you get.

It took a lot of work to get my daughter to feel comfortable with everything. It was a gradual process. She had watched *Parent Trap* I don't know how many times—she was doing all she could to try to sabotage us. Finally, I sat her down and told her, "You are going to have to accept this, it is going to happen." When she was around Ken, I would see that she was having a good time. Then she would realize she was having fun and go back to her little ways.

The wedding was the turning point. During the ceremony, after we said our vows, Ken presented Alana with a diamond cross. He put it around her neck and when she looked down, her face lit up like a Christmas tree. He made a little speech: "This is not just about your mother and me, it's about you as well. We are all a family." That solidified their relationship. I know that she is going to benefit from having a father in the household. She is going to benefit from having him in her life.

During the ceremony, the reverend said, "God doesn't like divorce. Divorce is bad. Promise you'll never get divorced." He made us promise. It's funny, because he's been divorced himself. I was like, "Okay, all right, I will not get divorced!" But I am glad he did it. When things get rough, I hope I remember that moment and say, "I promised, I will not get divorced." That will always stick with me.

BRUCE

If you had asked me twenty-five years ago, I certainly would not have expected to be marrying a man. Having a commitment ceremony was important for us as individuals, but perhaps more important to do in front of our families and friends. We have an absolute commitment to each other; this is not a "roommates plus" arrangement. We wanted to deal with our union openly and honestly.

Gay marriage forces a lot of family issues because it is not customary. It can bring the families together, and in the gay setting that is sometimes a challenge. There continues to be a certain stigma about it. I am thrilled that our parents have come as far as they have. My father is quite conservative. Rob's parents are deeply committed to the Catholic faith and this was a major, major step. I don't think every parent would dream of their kid having a gay marriage, but what our parents ultimately wanted was for us to be happy and safe and secure.

We wanted to have a grand event, to make a statement. Having the mayor perform the ceremony was not only symbolically important, but also at some level it would tell more skeptical family members that this is not something trite. The mayor is not going to participate in some goofball ceremony. There was this imprimatur from the mayor and the location that suggested that this is significant, and this marriage should be taken seriously.

Since we had the ceremony, I became part of Rob's family. Had we not done it I would have always been just his partner and now I am more than that. We made that public declaration, and we are stronger and closer to our families because of it. We are at ease; there is no hidden agenda. All the cards are out on the table.

TRACY

I had an aversion to marriage. My parents are divorced and most of my friends' parents are divorced. My experience with marriage was that it did not mean that much in my culture; the commitment was not there. When Tom asked me to marry him, I said, "I don't know, we have to think about it."

We talked about what marriage meant to us, and our commitment to each other. We wrote our entire ceremony. It was based on what we believed, not just the standard, unconscious wedding. I did not want to get married like that. I was symbolically uniting my life with his. That's why we picked the symbol of the braid. In the braid we each had our own thread, and there was a white thread, which represented the spirit of union. To me, marriage is about acknowledging that thread between us. If we stop weaving, our threads fall apart and there is nothing to hold us together. Marriage is not just about tying a knot. It's a living, daily, ongoing commitment. Each one of us brings our own thread to the braid. There are parts of our threads that are damaged, but if we want a strong union we have to be willing to remake it. Our weaving is a constant thing—we braid our lives together every day.

With our marriage, we added a new dimension to ourselves, but I did not want to give up my identity. It is important that I maintain my sense of self. I told Tom that I would never promise to be with him forever. That was like tying the knot and I could not say that; no one knows where life leads. I have committed to loving him and being the most present that I can be every day. If you live in the moment and you make those moments good, then you will be together forever.

CHRISTOPHER

I knew I wanted to get married. Amana was the one who always said, "Marriage is for pigs! Marriage is just a piece of paper, an institution handed down by the man!" Then, *suddenly*, almost overnight, it *all* changed, and she was like, "When are we going to get married?" Then there was all this pressure. She was getting dangerously close to delivering the "marriage ultimatum."

We wanted to have a massive celebration—completely out of control fun that was also elegant and fancy in a strange California way—and have a very legitimate ceremony that involved everybody yet felt intimate. We had over two hundred guests, but it felt like only a few people were there. We got married in a huge pine forest amongst the dried weeds of a California October. I was really persistent in my desire for a space in the woods.

I cried during our ceremony. I kept thinking that Amana was so pretty. I liked the bigness of all the trees. I took the time to look around, to smile at friends, to look at Amana, to check out everything that was going on. I was prepared to stop and ask if everyone could hear. It wasn't a movie, it wasn't a play. We weren't trying to create a staged scene. We didn't want people sitting in the back, spacing out, thinking, "Hey, what are they going to have for dinner?" We wanted people to be so intrigued with what we had to say that they would feel affected, like they had truly participated and not just watched.

When we walked back down the aisle, we could see the big smiles on everybody's faces. Finally, we got to turn and pay attention to everyone else. We saw all these people from different walks of our life, excited and happy, wiping their tears away and clapping. It could not have gotten any better at that point. When we left we were skipping down the road.

Being married not only implies the seriousness of our relationship, it also implies this move to adulthood. People perceive me differently since we married, even though I still wear the same holey T-shirts. We had been going out for ten years, but suddenly Amana is a legitimate member of my family, and I am a legitimate member of her family. Even our friends refer to us differently. There is a bit of irony that this ceremony, literally this piece of paper, makes our relationship official in other people's minds.

Everything feels a little more stable since we got married, a little more permanent, but not significantly different. You don't want it to be the *best* thing that is *ever* going to happen to you. You don't want it to be like your high school glory days where you're still talking about how you caught the touchdown pass twenty-six years ago. It was the greatest thing we had done up until that point, but now we are off on a new path.

"My mother said, 'Honey, no matter what, never withhold sex,' And she's still married, so she must not be doing that."

— JULAINE

JOANN

I had already planned five weddings—I never thought I would be planning my own. When my last child got married, I thought, "Thank God, they're all over with now." I certainly did not think of myself as the marrying type again. In the first place, I wasn't that young. I thought, "Who's going to look at me? I'm a grandmother."

I was coming out of my shell as far as grieving. We had just celebrated our forty-second anniversary when Jim died. I came from a very strong marriage. I married my high school sweetheart—I was only nineteen, a good little Catholic girl—and had five children by the age of thirty. I went from my parents' home to a home with my husband. I never had an interim period like young girls who go off to college and all.

About nine months after I lost Jim I had come to a point where I rather enjoyed my independence. I was going back in time to when I should have had that period. I had my own space and I was making my own decisions. I would go shopping and buy whatever I wanted. I was in a wonderful circle of friends. I really started playing. I knew I would always have activities. I was not one of these widows who would just be sitting around. I had this fantasy that it would be nice to know a couple of men to call on when I needed an escort. Marriage was not something I was concerned about.

But I was fascinated by Jack. I found myself always looking forward to seeing him, spending more time with him than I thought I would, working him into my schedule. I was surprised that I was enjoying his company so much. It was so natural with him. That is something that you can't even explain. The chemistry is either there or it isn't.

Once we were married, Jack seemed so relaxed about everything. I was shy. It took me a good six months of closing the doors and all that. He was still a stranger to me in that sense. Women think differently than men do. I thought to myself a few times that I was living with someone else's husband—almost like I was cheating on my first husband. That's gone now, but it took a few months. I wasn't quite sure what in the world I was doing.

Now he really is my husband. Those words were hard to say for a while. I am just getting to that point now, after eight months of marriage. He'll sometimes say, "In my previous life . . ." and I will put my hands to my ears and say, "No, I don't want to know anything about a previous life. You are my husband now and you never had another life."

"It was just a roller coaster of love."

— ZACH

HOBIE

My life story, before I met Gina, was that I was the brother, the son, who could never do anything right. People felt that I was totally lost in space, especially with my first marriage. What I felt standing up there was mixed. On one hand, I felt that I could say to these people who I had always imagined doubted me, "This is going to work." It felt great to have found such a wonderful woman. I felt like finally, I have done something these people can understand. But at the same time, I was nervous. "Do they think that Gina is as wonderful as I think she is? Are they as happy as I am?"

I wanted everybody in my life to know that I really love this woman and to see us get married. During our ceremony, when Gina and I were holding each other's hands and staring at each other, I felt, "This is it. Marrying Gina is going to change my life." I had been struggling for so many years—struggling, struggling, struggling. At that moment, I felt like my struggles were over.

In a lot of marriages, men don't get that you have to share everything. You don't just go earn a living and that's it. That's not fair, and it's not going to work. The man has to be prepared to do half of everything, to say, "Am I contributing fully to this relationship?" It's a lot of work—emotional work and also doing the laundry, doing the dishes, thinking about dinner, knowing how to make a bed. For me, having had a marriage that didn't work, it's important that I don't blow it.

ELLEN

We had so much immediate love for each other. We were creating art and poetry that were so over the top of anything we had ever done before. We were doing cartwheels on the beach and writing our names in the sand. We stayed out all night. It was very romantic. We were so close—it felt like we were breathing at the same time. I had this stir, that really excited feeling, which we called "bubbly-insideness." It was new, this love that we had. It was different. It immediately felt right. It had never felt so right.

Now I feel settled. I have found what I wanted to find. My ideas about marriage have changed over the years. I did not understand it when I first got married. I thought it was about that love and intense passion. Then I realized that marriage is hard. It takes a lot of work, yet it is a beautiful commitment. It is something I hope I can do forever because I deeply respect it. The intensity that we felt at first is obviously different now. I love Noel for that and so much more. I did not marry him for the father he is, and I lucked out. He is a great father. He is a great man. I sensed what he would be like, but I feel tremendously lucky to have gotten so much more than that initial passion. I want our marriage to last a lifetime. Marriage is a challenge, but it is the most exciting and romantic challenge that you can dive into.

KIM

I am very driven—all of my teachers used to tell me I was going to be the first woman president. I wanted to be something in life and for some reason, in my mind, that meant that I was not going to get married. I grew up in a family with seven kids, so kids did not seem that fun to me because they were always crying and taking my mom away. I did not get the whole family itch. As a kid, I said I was never going to get married.

When I met Zach I realized I could be great and do everything I wanted, and have him. He makes life easier. My mom has had people come up to her and say, "Oh, what a shame! Kim was always so smart." Society thinks that life ends for a girl after marriage and I have realized that is not true at all. I have not stopped my life because I am married. To me, marriage is deciding that you are going to work hard at a relationship and that you are going to put that relationship first, before work, before everything. Being married doesn't mean that I can't be successful.

Now that we are married, everything seems simultaneously more serious and more laughable. Things are serious, but all those little things that used to bother us don't anymore because we know we are going to be together forever.

JASON

It was love at first sight; my heart went pitter-patter. It was literally that *click*. Less than a month later we were engaged. It was not my plan to become married at the age of twenty-five. I was going to go off and become a big war correspondent–journalist. I had no interest in getting married, or being in a serious relationship. Half the people I knew were divorced—everything was pushing me away from marriage. But it was such a compelling thing that there was no stopping it.

I didn't even intend to propose. It happened over the phone. We were having one of those conversations about how much we loved being together. I was rambling on and on about how wonderful it was to have her in my life, and I said, "I can see that you are the person I want to be with for the rest of life. Will you marry me?" And she said, "Okay." Then we were stuck. What do you do at that point? You just go through with it. It was just the way it was going to be. That was twelve years ago.

I always ask people if they feel different after they get married. Some people say no, and I am always surprised. I felt a finality—we closed one chapter and opened up another in a very significant way. I had the feeling that I couldn't walk away from this, and I didn't want to. The apprehension and uncertainty of whether things were going to continue was gone.

People fear looking vulnerable or failing in front of the person that they love, but the thing that is going to get you through is to lay it bare. The fact that they still like you when you let down your masks is a testament to their loving you. If you have those walls, then forget it. There is nothing that Sarah doesn't know about me. Marriage keeps you from being too self-absorbed. It manages your sense of ego, because you are always going to have somebody who will tell you that you are full of it, but at the same time they will tell you they love you. Being married has taught me a lot about being a good person.

There are these fleeting moments, more and more fleeting as we get older, when she looks at me and I know that she absolutely loves me. I am getting fat and wrinkly and ugly and my wife still wants to make love to me, probably only because she is seeing me with twenty-five-year-old eyes. She says, "I still love you like the day I married you, when you were handsome." That is an awfully amazing feeling.

LEANNE

As the "best woman," I had to be moral support for my friend and the party coordinator as well. It was a huge responsibility. On the wedding day, both of the mothers wanted to be in charge. It was hard for the groom's mother not to be in total control of absolutely everything. A conflict was arising. I saw this, so I took over. Where one mom wanted to be in control, I said to her, "No, no that's my job." The same with the other. I would say, "No, I'm gonna take care of that, you enjoy yourselves today." It avoided a lot of friction, especially between the bride and her mother-in-law.

At the end of the wedding, all the boys were out smoking cigars—they were proud and happy that their pal had gotten hooked up. Usually, it is the men's ritual of celebration in a wedding, but I was not afraid to smoke a big fat cigar, and to take an hour smokin' it. I needed a little rest. I was too busy to smoke a cigar when I was running around making everything happen. I had a sense of relief when it was over. It was an overwhelming day.

GEORGE

The notion of a formal wedding was a big obstacle for both of us. We had to start from scratch. Our wedding was entirely different from what I had imagined. I grew up Catholic, so I envisioned the church that we went to when I was a kid with the long aisle and high ceilings. I envisioned the bride in white with the father walking her up the aisle. It's not that I expected my wedding to be that way, I just assumed it would be that way. It's such a convention that I couldn't see it any other way. I am thankful that Jane did not want that because we ended up with much more than I had expected.

The traditional notion is that the man is supposed to let the woman do what she wants. There are some weddings where the bride wants to take control and the groom can't give any input, and there are times when the bride has to take control because the groom doesn't give any input. I would say to any man who is getting married, "You should be involved! This is your wedding! This is your marriage!"

When I woke up the morning of the wedding, the first thing I did was run to the window and look out, like a little kid going to Disneyland. It was a perfect blue sky, not a cloud up there. I was like, "Oh my God, this is perfect!" Everything from that point on was kind of a blur.

After I got dressed, I went up to see Jane and it was amazing—she was so beautiful. I remember thinking, "Now I understand why people who see their bride-to-be every day would think that she is the most beautiful woman in the world at that particular moment." It was the realization of what we were about to do together.

We went downstairs and looked outside. There were so many people out there, crowded around the little aisle in our backyard. We walked forward and everything went so quickly. The ceremony was short and powerful. It was important to stand up in front of everybody and make that commitment. When we walked back down the aisle everyone was looking at us. All of our friends and family looked so happy—they were all smiling at us. For one minute, it was all about us. I was ecstatic. That day was the happiest day of my life until now.

AMBER

I never realized how amazing weddings are until I had one. They are about love. You get people together who would never get together otherwise. My family would never be in the same room unless there was a graduation or somebody died. This time it was different—at our wedding nobody fought, people ate and danced. Everyone was so happy.

The ceremony worried me because it wasn't religious. I didn't want people to show up and say, "Well, what are we doing here?" I was concerned about what I was going to say to Sonja because I wanted my words to be symbolic of all the things that I was feeling. I felt a lot of pressure to say the right thing. Then I started to wonder, am I more worried about what people are going to think or are we doing this because we want to? Thinking about where is everyone going to sit, is my family going to get along, am I going to get along with my mother? All those pressures can make you forget that your wedding is not about them, it is about you.

In some ways, I just could not believe we were doing it. Right before we were going down the aisle I thought, "I don't know, I don't know!" I wanted to leave; I was petrified. I wanted to get in the car and drive away. It is such an intimate experience—you are baring your soul for all those people to see. It makes you feel vulnerable. You do it in front of other people to make your commitment stronger, but it is so intimate that you almost don't want people to be there.

The wedding is supposed to be the bride's day—without a groom you have two brides sharing the same spotlight. Who do you look at, who do you say is beautiful? I was glad there was another bride up there with me. We both looked beautiful.

PAUL

People have a concept of the perfect person. It's a fairy tale. For guys, often it is some gorgeous babe who is a combination of slut and angel—always beautiful, always fun, someone who takes care of him and at the same time looks great on his arm. You can get wrapped up in this idea and so you go from girl to girl to girl looking for that. Women have the "Prince Charming syndrome." When you first meet someone, you put your image of what you think this person should be on top of who they are. You go, "Man, this is so exciting and great." When they do something that steps outside of this mold, all of a sudden the whole image shatters. Marriage is letting go of your preconceptions, accepting there is no Mister or Miss Perfect, transcending those shallow things to get to something deeper.

I got married late, in my forties. I had let relationships happen as opposed to consciously making decisions about what I was looking for. I would meet someone who was attracted to me and suddenly I would be in a relationship. I knew that if I didn't make some serious changes in how I think, this in and out of relationships could go on forever. There was a lot of pain in the process, but I wanted to make a commitment and settle down. I knew what I was looking for. It was a very conscious thing. It took one more try, but I got it right.

The preparation for marriage started before I met Peggy. I struggled with the thought, "You're going to marry this person and this is it—for the rest of your life." I tried to accept that finality. There was resistance to jumping in. Marriage had always been this very serious thing that other people did. But I knew that was what I wanted. The little voice inside of me was the old voice that would have me going back on the old path. I had to tell it to shut up and say, "I know this is right."

Marriage is a partnership. I am not able to do things single-mindedly. I was used to living hand to mouth for years. Nobody other than my parents complained about when I was going to get a real job. If I wanted to eat Top Ramen for a week, I'd eat Top Ramen for a week. But now, it's not the same. Peggy has become my family. We are building a life together. I can't imagine the world without her.

"My husband and I were given very different advice from our grandparents before getting married. My grandfather said that you cannot go to sleep in a fight—stay up until you have worked it out. And my husband was given the advice that there's nothing that won't be better in the morning—just sleep on it."

— LIZ

SLOANE

Your wedding is the day you have to proclaim your love and have a spotlight on the relationship. I looked forward to that. We wanted a big, outdoor, fun extravaganza. No one was telling us what to do, so we just planned it ourselves, without worry. Our wedding came out of who we are very naturally. Nick's father was in the front row rolling his eyes and holding his head because he saw all these funny moments.

We had a children's parade with an accordion player—there were probably twenty-five kids there. Everybody wrote a wish or a hope for our marriage and tied it to a prayer stick. One friend burned sage to make a clean space, to clear the air. Nobody on the East Coast had seen this. Everyone was freaking out because they thought we were setting fire to something. Another friend was calling to the four directions, which is a way to draw attention to nature around us. We had a judge because we didn't want to have a religious ceremony—we didn't feel we needed God sanctioning the marriage. We wrote the vows ourselves, using "to have and to hold until death do us part," and adding other parts that were more naturalistic. They were somewhat traditional vows in an otherwise untraditional setting.

I don't know why I had a white dress, but I'm glad I did. I felt if I dressed the part it would be an important day, a special day. I thought of all the wedding pictures I had seen over the years, and they were always such beautiful pictures. I imagined myself in those same photos. I was not going to lose that. We had no ice sculpture, no limousines, no video camera at the wedding. Nick's dog was the ring bearer. That upset his brother, who was his best man. Nick had several conversations with him so he would not feel he was being upstaged by a dog. We thought it would be funny to whistle and have the dog run up the aisle. We got a special little necklace for her, and of course she is such a well-trained dog that she performed perfectly on cue.

ED

I wasn't looking to get married, but I started thinking about my age. I thought, "I'm fifty-two, what am I going to do for the next twenty-five years? Am I going to be a bachelor or what?" I kept hearing that people live longer if they're married. I didn't want to be by myself anymore.

When I told my youngest son, he said, "Dad, you are insane. Why are you doing this?" He thought of me as the eternal bachelor. I had told him that I would never get married again because of the bad time I had with my divorce from my first marriage. But all of that callous thinking wore out. I said, "Yeah, I may be a little crazy, but I know what I'm doing."

Lucky is very Catholic, so she was the first to say we were living in sin and we should think seriously about getting married. I thought about it for a while and agreed, especially with our baby coming along. Lucky wanted to get married in the church, but they had a six-month waiting period. After she had a miscarriage, I wanted to get married right away, before the end of the year. I said, "Let's get married at city hall. If we want to get married in a church, we can do that later." The religious ceremony is mostly to make Lucky happy. She considers the civil ceremony just a legal thing, although it turned out better than we expected. With a religious wedding, she will feel officially married. She thinks that if you don't do it in a church, it's not going to be right.

BETH

I got to a point where I didn't want to just be dating people here and there. I was thirty-seven years old and I needed to move forward in my life. I was thinking, "What's wrong with me? Why haven't I found my match yet?" I would look at others who were married and having children—it seemed like they were moving forward in their lives, and I was going round and round in a circle. I was stuck in this single-dating-gal phase. I was starting to lose hope. I was thinking, "I am just going to be an old cat lady." I was very ripe for meeting the right person. I wanted to find my perfect match, and to have a family.

Before we got married I felt committed, there was no question about it. The wedding was just a high point in our relationship. It felt a little surreal, like, "Wow! This is a special day. This is our wedding day. But it's a regular day. I'm eating a bowl of cereal." It had this contradictory feeling of regular ol' things happening and very special moments.

I didn't know how fun our wedding was going to be. I didn't know I was going to feel these deep emotions, the deep feeling of love. I thought we were going to have a nice time, we were going to get married. But the love and joy and celebration were incredible. I was caught up in a swirl of fun and excitement. No wonder people have weddings. Now I understand! Brides always say, "This is the best day of my life." I used to think, "Eh! That's cliché." But it really was one of the best days of my life.

I felt so in love with Artie. When we drove off on our honeymoon, we were overwhelmed with feelings of love. We were both crying. We would just look at each other and our eyes would fill with tears. It was so fun to say "husband" and "wife," and look at the ring and think, "Oh my gosh! There's my hand with the ring." I loved that anybody on the street could look at my hand and see that, yes, I was married. It was a feeling of pride. I found a great mate and I wanted everyone to know. I loved that all of a sudden he was my husband. It felt good to have a word that reflected our relationship in a more honest, appropriate way. I had finally realized all of the hopes and wishes that I couldn't express for fear that I wouldn't get married. It was like a sigh of relief and joy.

"You have to take each other seriously, but you can't take *yourself* too seriously."

—AMANA

DAVID

We were set up on a blind date and we totally hit it off. About forty-five minutes into dinner, I imagined that we were in a Lamaze class together and I was helping her give birth. I had never even entertained the thought before. Of course, I didn't tell her that. The next day I told a friend about it and he said that he would have run out of there so fast and thrown a hand grenade over his shoulder just so that thought never came up again.

We were headed toward marriage, and then a year and a half into the relationship we got pregnant. A friend of mine had asked us a week before we found out, "What would you guys do if you got pregnant?" I said, "It certainly would make things easier, we wouldn't have to make any choices." I still had a lot of commitment-phobia. It was a wake-up call. I thought, "If we are serious about this then we are going to be together forever."

When I was twenty-five or so I probably had a very unrealistic view of marriage in that I thought it should be up all the time, like a Pepsi ad or something. By the time I got married I had become much more realistic about what it meant. I see marriage as a lifelong commitment, but not a life sentence. It's too easy to throw in the towel—that is one reason why I am glad I didn't do it earlier. Now, the idea of getting a divorce seems so painful and awkward. I know that if I did get divorced, I would just be trading for different baggage with somebody else.

Being married allows you to let go of checking out other possibilities in terms of relationships. When you are dating, you are constantly negotiating. You can have one foot out the back door. But when you are committed, you settle into appreciating the person and not questioning it so much. We have agreed to take this shared journey together: to support each other, to be the best people that we can be as a couple, and to continue to nurture the relationship.

T

We dated for nine years and we always thought we were going to get married, but we said when the time comes, we'll just know. I never worried much about it. One day it came to me, like a voice from the blue: "It is time now." It was one of the few moments in my life when I felt absolutely, no question, this is perfect.

I wanted to surprise her, even though we had talked about how we would mutually arrive at this decision. I set the whole thing up in my head. I wanted to propose on the beach where we'd had this magical kiss years before. I was trying to get her to walk down to this place and she didn't want to go for a walk at all. I browbeat her into going with me and she was grumpy the whole time. When we got to the spot, I took the ring out of my pocket and got down on one knee. I had actually practiced that by myself in my apartment, getting down on my knee, because I wanted to make sure I wasn't going to fall over on my face and make a fool of myself. I was thinking, "Okay, right knee goes forward, left knee goes down." I took out the ring and said, "Will you marry me?"

She turned around and basically shrieked and backed away from me. "What? Why didn't you talk to me about this first?" That was her response. I said, "Come on Leslie, I'm on my knee here." I was sort of shuffling after her on my knee as she was backing away from me, saying "Come on, come on."

I was rather disappointed that she wasn't ecstatic. She wasn't bubbly or overflowing with enthusiasm. She was thinking about it. It wasn't like the proposal was this great, shining, glorified moment. We both realized the gravity of what we were about to do. Once you enter into it, it is forever. That is probably one reason we didn't get married when we were twenty-five. It is a huge commitment.

You always hear about little girls wanting to grow up and get married, but I dreamed of it, too. My parents have a great marriage. They always talk about how they have loved having kids and being married. I looked forward to that; I knew it would be a good thing. Marriage has been what I thought it would be—it is wonderful and fulfilling.

LISELI

I was one of those kids who was designing her wedding gown in eighth grade. My wedding was going to be simple and elegant, but I never thought about the logistics. I didn't actually think about creating an event for a hundred people. I just imagined myself; a big, white, fluffy dress; some random guy; and my family. That was my idea of a wedding.

Money was a primary concern. We could have done it on a shoe-string budget, which is what I wanted, something simple. But then you have family to consider, all these people you *have* to invite. It is a once in a lifetime thing, people are flying from all over the world to be here for us, we have to make it nice. It was tough, juggling both families and the money and all the rest of it. Now I understand why everyone says it's one of the most stressful times. There are so many things you have to juggle, so many different people's ideas and needs and wants.

We wanted our wedding to be low-key but elegant. It was important that people danced and had a good time. A wedding has to be about dancing. I was brought up in Peru and Zambia, and in Latin and African culture it is all about the dancing. Everybody was on the dance floor and having a good time. Brian's aunt, who I had met only at these formal family occasions, was starting a conga line. Our grandmothers were out there, too. It was a side of his family that I never get to see.

People kept saying, "What a fun wedding," as opposed to, "What a beautiful wedding." That's not something that I thought about when I was young. I didn't think about people having fun, it just needed to look good—everything was supposed to be beautiful and perfect. But the fact that everyone had such a good time was unexpected and wonderful.

NUME

I was thinking about marriage and at the same time turning thirty. My parents were talking to me about settling down. Julie never pressured me, but she did give me hints here and there. She wanted to be married to me. It was up to me to make the next move because she was ready. I felt that if I didn't act soon she might be gone. She just made me realize what I needed and wanted to do.

Everybody gave me advice. They tried to prep me for it, to make sure I knew what I was getting into, having a woman come into my life. You hear it, but you don't really understand until you go through it yourself. I had a tough time letting go of my friends and my freedom. There were times when I would do things on my own and not think about her. I was a little selfish at first. I had to straighten myself out. I knew that my friends would always be there and they would understand that I wouldn't be able to see them whenever I wanted. My wife has to come first. I knew that was part of the sacrifice. I was ready.

I have more responsibilities now being the head of the household and having a wife. It has been a big change in many ways. I just know that this is the woman I love, and I am going do whatever it takes to make it work.

JULAINE

As soon as the ceremony was over we were rocking and rolling. Everyone was sweating, dancing, rocking out. The whole floor was shaking. The band was going, everyone was getting into it. Then the bandleader got all the guys in a circle and said, "Okay, pull out a dollar from your wallet and stick it into your belt, like this." It was flapping over their front zippers. Then it dawned on me, "Oh, man, what have I gotten myself into? This is going to be mortifying!" I went up to him and asked, "What are you going to make me do?" He said, "You don't have to do anything, dear!" I was like, "Oh, okay."

The dance had all of these hip movements. It was "one cent" off to the left, "five cents" off to the right, "ten cents" throw your booty back, and then "dollar" was the pelvic thrust. I was in the middle of all these guys and they were going left, right, back, and "dollar!" At one point the song goes, "Dollar! Dollar! Dollar!"

The bandleader took the first few dollars, then he said, "Okay—you go, girl!" He turned me loose. I was thinking to myself, "Oh my God, what is Stefan's mother going to think?" I suffered with trepidation through the first few. But halfway around the circle I was like, "Whatever, let's go for it!" I thought his relatives were going to be horrified, but everyone was just laughing. Nobody was like, "Who is this vulgar floozy?" It was a bit bawdy, but fun. When I finally made it around the circle I was like, "Yes! I did it!"

JONATHAN

I was on a total high our whole wedding day. From the moment I woke up in the morning until the next day there was this sense of great energy and calm and excitement, all at the same time. It was a fantastic feeling. There was great love all around us. We had this community of friends and family who were just glowing. It was contagious. It felt like we could do no wrong, there could be no wrong in the world. I walked through the day six inches off the ground. I wasn't worried about anything. I was surrounded by my cadre, my men in arms. People were going all out, celebrating.

Getting married was a wonderful feeling. It was thrilling, but at the same time very calming. I felt more grounded and sure of myself than at any other time in my life. I had this high, this sense of euphoria. I think it was about knowing that Sarah and I were going to spend the rest of our lives together. We were so excited. We were totally in love. Knowing that our union was being celebrated by everybody that we cared about was sublime.

STACY

My job as a wedding-gown designer made what I wore both more important and less important at the same time. Since that is my job, I knew everyone would be looking at my dress—and I wanted to have a beautiful gown. At the same time, I realized how insignificant the wedding gown is. I had seen so many women place way too much importance on the gown, like it was the be-all, end-all. I was pregnant, so I had to give up on my original plan, and as a result it took on even less importance to me. It became a very simple dress.

Growing up you have all of these fantasies about how you want your wedding to look and where you want it to be, all these material things, but you don't grasp the emotional and spiritual significance of it until you are there. During the process of getting married your priorities change. The dress and flowers become much less significant and the meaning of the ceremony becomes more significant. When we were up there saying our vows I was not aware of anybody around us; all I was aware of was the words of our ceremony and what they meant to us. We were proclaiming our love and devotion to each other in front of everybody. That was what really mattered.

MARK

I called my father when John and I got engaged. He was supportive, to a degree. He was glad I had a partner, but he did not say much about this wedding business. He had to internalize the whole notion that his son was getting married to a man. I knew that he had finally accepted it when we were talking a few months later and out of the blue he said, "You are not going to wear white jackets with ruffled shirts, are you?" I said, "What?" He said, "At your wedding, you are not going to wear matching white, ruffly things, are you?" I said, "No, we probably will not wear anything matching. We are going to wear something tasteful." He said, "Okay, fine. I was just a little worried."

I realized he had come to grips with our getting married when his biggest concern was that we were somehow going to do it in poor taste. That was a big hurdle for my dad. We were blessed that all of our immediate family came, without exception. They were overjoyed to be there, even though we did not wear ruffled shirts, neither of us wore a dress, and there was no drag.

My love, my respect, my awe for John increased a zillionfold on our wedding day. He stood up and said all those things to me, made all those declarations in front of all those people. Yes, I already knew he loved me, I knew he was committed to me, but he did it. He did the act, which means he meant it all. I am so grateful. Nothing else can say "I love you" like saying "I love you" in front of your friends and family—saying, "I really love you, forever."

Everyone wants to say getting married does not change anything, but it does. I get to say "husband," which is really a great thing to say. No matter how you slice it, even if it is a gay relationship and you have the weirdness of it being two guys, nothing conveys better what someone means to you than the word "husband." That term means someone for whom you have made that commitment, done that crazy thing in front of your family and friends. There is no way you can say "significant other" or "boyfriend" or "my guy" or "my man." Nothing else does it. There is great power in using the word "husband."

"At ten o'clock, everything changes. Nothing changes, but everything changes."

—JASON

DE

I have always been very choosy. I am almost forty and this is my first marriage. I waited so long because I wanted to be sure. No one can be absolutely sure, but I wanted it to be just once. It never felt right before. This feels right. I know that I want to spend my life with her. It is not mathematics, it is not science. It is like jazz: You know it's good but you don't know why.

MIKE

That dance was one of the most incredible five minutes of my life. We didn't know what was going to happen. We picked out the song, and practiced a couple times on our living room floor. We thought, "Oh, that's pretty good. We can do that." But in no way did I expect the magnitude of what went on there. It was so magical—the music, the dance, the reaction of the crowd. I could see people out of the corner of my eye, and they were going nuts. They all had the face that I did. It was just a super high. Leslie was so happy. It was the greatest wedding I have ever been to and it will probably never be matched.

As a father-in-law I had not one minute of doubt that they were perfect for each other—that he was going to take care of her and I'd never have to worry about her ever again. I don't expect them ever to have marital problems or get divorced or anything. It just cannot happen. It was too magical.

BREANN

I didn't think that I was the kind of person who was going to settle down. I viewed marriage as some really adult step; it never seemed like a viable possibility for me. Maybe I thought I didn't deserve to have an untroubled relationship. But it happened despite my best efforts to keep intimacy at bay.

I love to put on a show and the whole idea of the wedding was, "It's a party!" People didn't know until they got there just what we were up to. I thought our invitations were a giveaway, especially the ones where Timothy was half naked and had mouse ears on. It was a costumed idea. It was this absurd thing where I was putting on the wedding dress and Timothy was putting on the monkey suit. Looking like cake-toppers from some kind of tattoo bar, that's what I wanted. People know us as being very eccentric so we had to live up to that, too—our wedding could not have been the average city hall thing.

I did not have that little-girl idea of the white-wedding-marriage-cake thing—even though of course there was a white dress and there was cake involved—but that is not something I chased down and beat into submission. The props and costumes that I was comfortable with were teasing some very somberly held ideals about what weddings ought to be. Costume was extremely important. People associate the wedding dress with a million things all at once, but ultimately it's instantly recognizable in our culture: "Look, there is the bride—the virginal princess!" There is just this love-bombing going on because you are wearing that gown.

The flames were my antidote to the overt, unbreakable tradition. I was obsessed with the idea of the suffering motif—the woman in flames is an image that speaks to me. That goes back to my distorted view of myself, especially prior to Timothy's entering my life, as being a tortured, misunderstood, complicated person. "Who can touch me? I am in my own hell."

When it came down to the one-on-one thing, that's where it got super-intense. I was freaking out when I was literally there in front of him. Suddenly it was so real. It was no longer the costumes and all the fun we had in preparing for the wedding. I was surprised at how raw I felt. I was overwhelmed with emotion. Whether you are a traditionalist or doing something with a holy lama in some tropical place, you are saying something. You are speaking from your soul. Everything else could disappear. It is just you two, that contract, that agreement.

You can have a relationship and be totally committed and live together for years and years and years, but when you say those words aloud, "I do," it is like a little Ziploc bag—it seals the deal. Timothy and I had been together for years and we had lived together; it had been an established relationship. But it was new, in a sense. We had given ourselves license to call it a new thing.

Even though I mock some of the ideals of love and commitment because I have a sarcastic nature, this was a high-water mark in my life. It was important to me to be able to stand up and proudly say, "I love Timothy." I don't have a great track record as far as relationships go. By far this is my Olympic record, and Timothy is my gold medal.

SONJA

Marriage is about saying, "I am going to be there when it is crappy." It is not always going to be good, there is so much that is not going to work out. I have seen my parents go through a lot of crap in their marriage and stay together. It is about that commitment. The good stuff—the love, getting along, the happy times—that is all a given. That's the easy part. You don't say, "I want to be with you forever because it is all going to be great." To me it is saying, "I want to be with you to work through this stuff. I am there." That's what marriage is. Whether it was the paper or our saying to all of the people who have spanned huge parts of our lives, "This is the person I am with, and we want your support."

The fact that I wanted to have a traditional wedding was weird to me because there was never any expectation to do that. My parents were completely thrilled when I told them. They liked Amber and wondered if I was going to settle down. It made my mom come out about me to all their friends. I was not going to go to them and say, "Hey, I am a lesbian." All of her friends were fine. They knew. I am thirty and here I am with girlfriend number four who has come home for the holidays. They were like, "Yeah, we get it." Once their friends knew, they could talk freely. They didn't have to make up stories. My mom could say, "We are planning the wedding."

The father-daughter dance really sticks out in my mind. Amber and her dad were kind of going wild, they were so out there. My dad and I are very conventional. We were just dancing and talking. My dad looked over and said, "I don't dance like that. I guess I'm the conservative one." I said, "I think I am, too." It very much defined who we are. He told me, a couple of times, "I love you so much." He said, "I am really happy for you and I hope that you are happy. What you have done today was so wonderful. I hope you work and honor this commitment to each other." Our families definitely respect our relationship. We are a single unit now.

Marriage is very grounding for me. I have a sense of peace. I can go out and no matter what happens during my day, I know I have this person who I can come home to. You wear so many different hats during the day—it is nice to just come home and have one person who lets you be yourself.

"For a lot of people, single life is the anomaly. You grow up in a household where you see a relationship and you are part of a family. Then you go off on your own and finally get your independence. Eventually, you realize that being part of a family is not a bad thing. You left home to make your own way but in the end, what you want is home."

—RUSS

KIM

Three days before the wedding I had the final dress fitting, the practice run. I put on the dress and the veil, and I felt so ugly. I cried and cried and cried. My mom was trying to calm me down. I was stressed. I felt like there was so much pressure to look a certain way and have the day be a certain way. It was the biggest day of my life. We were spending so much money and it was going to be captured in photographs that we would have sitting on our office desks for years to come—so much of this one day would live on in people's minds forever.

I had gotten sick the morning of our wedding, and I was ready to faint that afternoon. I had not eaten anything. I couldn't even smile right. I felt like I was going to cry just from nerves. I did not have the bubbly warm emotions everyone hopes to get on their wedding day. It was supposed to be this day when I felt wonderful, but I didn't feel that everything inside of me was coming together. I wasn't nervous about getting married at all, I was just worried about the big show. Maybe that's what weddings do—they take your mind completely off of what you are actually doing. The most important thing about a wedding is that two people are getting married, but that can get lost in the shuffle.

One person came up to me and said, "Look around, try to memorize this. This is your day, this is everything you have been working for." It was like, "Oh yeah, I am actually supposed to enjoy myself, too." I feel like I missed it. After all the time that I put into choosing everything and making it what I wanted it to be, I got there and I didn't see it. I was so busy saying "Hi" to everyone and doing everything that a bride is supposed to do. It was a long checklist on the day of the wedding—I was busy trying to check everything off that list.

Looking back, my wedding did turn out to be the best day of my life, even though it was hard to see that at the time. I am super happy being married, and I got a great party favor—Zach!

SARAH

Getting married—the actual wedding planning—forces a couple to examine all of the issues: family, money, religion. It is a big test. It took a certain amount of letting go on both of our parts. It taught us how to be a couple.

I went into it thinking that we would make it our own wedding, do it our own way and be unconventional. But I realized that I was in the machinations of a ritual that went beyond what I wanted. It was about what people expected and being accommodating to them. Once I had the epiphany that my wedding was not actually about me, but about making everyone else happy, it became a lot easier.

Getting married—the actual marriage part—is learning how to think as a couple, creating that new family. I had been an "I" for a long time, and that was the beginning of the forging of a "we." It is hard work, that transition. I often think that instead of giving people a wedding present, I should give them a therapy fund. The first year of marriage is really hard. We had never lived together, so we had a lot of hashing out to do. I remember thinking, "This is why you get married, so you can't get out of it easily. That piece of paper is going to make me work this out right now, damn it!"

Now when we have hard times, we are so together that it's not a question at all. We have been through so much in just five years. I can only imagine us getting closer. We have a primitive, deep connection. Jonathan has saved my life so many times. I truly believe that he can save me from anything.

AMANA

We knew that we wanted our wedding to be fun—that was our top priority. We had been to many weddings that were beautiful and perfect to the eye, but they were not fun. Our goal was to have people turn toward each other at the wedding and say, "This is so Christopher and Amana. This is something only they could come up with."

It seemed like such a blessing that everyone we loved was together in one place, with so much good energy. The band was so goofy, they lit the place on fire. The first song was "1999," and we immediately ran for the dance floor. We were lucky that we did because every table cleared within two seconds and we were completely mobbed. That was the only moment that we were on our dance floor alone. We didn't have any official dances. There was no slow dancing at any time. Our friends whom we had assigned to do the "glam table" immediately popped up wearing outrageous outfits and tried to get all the old men to wear glow sticks and put body glitter on their faces and chests.

People flipped out—they were very fired up. Christopher was crowd surfing. Our friends were doing the inch worm. There was a time when we were actually in the inflatable bouncy castle with the lead singer while he was singing. It was total chaos by midnight. Things got out of control, everyone was in the pool and the music was going nuts. We had noise complaints from five miles away. The party was everything we wanted it to be—the food and the band and the silliness and the drinking and the bouncy castle and the cops at the dessert table, all of that blends into this big mirage. It felt like we were all little kids again, and that is exactly the way we wanted it.

LIZ

I never quite knew who I was going to be when I got married. I did not imagine myself getting married in a big, poofy white dress. I was happy that I did, but there wasn't some whole lifelong fantasy about that. Who I married was a big part of it. Dan wanted a traditional wedding, so that made me want to wear a real wedding dress. The wedding was the product of the two of us, it wasn't just the bride's prerogative for the entire thing. He insisted we have a cake. I didn't care about the wedding cake, but he was like, "Are you kidding? We are having a wedding cake. I want the experience of cutting my wedding cake at my wedding." I was not going to deny him that experience. Dan is much more romantic about these things than I am.

We did not want a secular ceremony. We wanted God to be invoked, which was a little surprising given that our specific religions are not all that important to either of us. We learned that they were in ways that we had not realized. I feel Jewish and I wanted to have a Jewish wedding. It was important to me not to close the door on that part of my life just because I was marrying someone who was not Jewish.

I wanted to get married under a huppah. I wanted Dan to break the glass. I wanted to circle him, which is a weird, slightly pagan thing. It is like casting a spell on your husband; it's very beautiful. We did the chair dance, which is a lovely tradition. People circle around and do a dance. Then they lift you up on the chairs. You have to literally let go and accept that your brother is not going to drop you. I felt like I was on a ride. The whole experience was joyous and exuberant.

Neither of us had any doubts. We both felt like, "You're the person I want to spend my life with, there is no one else out there for me." It really did feel like I was going off on a new adventure and starting a whole new phase of my life. Dan felt like my nuclear family in a way that I hadn't quite expected. When I was single, it was *so* much work just to take care of myself. I was tired—it was exhausting. I never feel like that anymore. I am not in the world alone.

NICK

As a child I always expected a more conventional wedding. I expected that I would concede to the desires of my family as I had conceded on almost everything in my life until then on major issues. I felt proud that I was able to create a wedding that reflected my values and was different from the conventional wedding that was planned for me all along.

The whole ceremony felt incredible, like we were entering a special, magical moment that I had always dreamed of. It was as perfect and blissful as I could have ever imagined. There was joy, but the tingling of nervousness carried through. I had never made a commitment to do anything this long in my entire life. I cried because of the delight of being there, all my love for Sloane, and also that it didn't rain. I felt sadness and happiness—it was a defining moment that would forever move me into the next stage of my life.

ASHA

That was my last time to say good-bye—my final good-bye—to my family. That is when it really hit me emotionally that I am married. I am going into his side of the family; they are my family now, that is where I have to be concerned. I have to watch what I say and do with them. I have to leave my family—now Rakesh's family comes first. It was all hitting me at once. Before it was just Rakesh and me, but at that moment I realized, "Wow, I have to take on his whole family as my responsibility."

NANCY

I was so unprepared for love; I was unprepared for knowing what was right. I remember when I was twelve or thirteen talking to a girlfriend's mother and saying, "I'm never going to get married. I'm just going to have affairs." I never envisioned marriage—the white dress, walking down the aisle. Who would ever want me?

Years later, Michael and I were sitting on the couch watching a baseball game and the words just came flying out of my mouth—"Will you marry me?" And he said, "Yes." That was it. It was very unromantic and at the same time it was ultimately romantic because it was so spontaneous and honest. There was no pretext, there was no planning. It was just a very open, raw expression of love.

My father was thrilled that we were getting married because finally there would be someone to take care of me. My mother was concerned that Michael didn't make enough money. I had gone through graduate school. I was an attorney. I thought, "You have absolutely no faith in your own daughter!" I know it's generational, but the message I was getting was that I'm not complete unless I have a guy. I am sure my brother never got that message.

I chose to wear my mother's wedding dress. Women wear their mothers' wedding gowns and I wanted to wear my mom's wedding suit. Later I wished I'd had a beautiful white gown. I don't know why. We were married outside in a field. It didn't feel right to have a white gown on at the time—my mom's suit just seemed right.

When I got dressed, all the little girls were oohing and aahing around me, murmuring, "Ooh, the bride!" It was so sweet. My cousin came in and said, "You look beautiful!" I have never thought of myself as a glamorous person by any means, but I felt good that day. It was like, "Oh yeah, I'm the bride! Look, I am all dressed up. I have my fancy clothes on and here we go."

During our ceremony, a full moon came up that was absolutely phenomenal. It gave an amazing warmth to the entire event. Being outside was important to us, having nature around us. There we were, in this beautiful space surrounded by open fields and trees and this unbelievable moon.

There's an idea that the wedding is going to change everything, that this one moment of this one day is the most important moment of our lives. It's not. Weddings don't necessarily change things. They are just the beginning of a new sameness. Hopefully, you continue to grow and evolve, but it's not like all of a sudden I became a different person. There is always that dreamy thought that everything is going to be blissful and lovely and roses and honey. But even in those times of daydreaming blissfully, there is a realization that this is life—life is hard, life gives you unexpected things. Marriage is hard. Marriage is great.

"The one thing that I found very amusing was that once you get married you're thinking that finally people are going to stop asking, 'When are you going to get married?' and then within a half hour they are asking, 'When are you going to have children?'"

—MICHAEL

ACKNOWLEDGMENTS

Unveiled has truly been a collaborative effort. The generous participation of these brides, grooms, and their families, and their willingness to divulge intimate thoughts on marriage has resulted in an illuminating look at commitment. Their tales have inspired me in countless ways. I cannot begin to thank them enough. There were some interviews I was unable to use, but every story was crucial in shaping my overall perspective on marriage and ultimately this book. I thank each and every one. I also want to thank the families, friends, and guests who appear in the photos for allowing me to use images that depict their best—and sometimes less flattering—sides.

None of this would have been possible without help from my interns Rita Badalamenti, Corwin Dormire, Patsy Eagan, Lauren Hammerschlag, Anisha Narasimhan, Aimée Reed, Seth Schwartz, Rania Sutton-Elbers, and Kate Weigel. In exchange for Mexican food and chocolates they printed hundreds of photographs, transcribed hours of interviews, helped edit excerpts and images, contributed significant insights, and lifted my spirits every day.

Very special thanks to many friends who offered emotional and practical support, particularly Jennifer Blake, Carol Clark, Amy Douglas, Ed Kashi, Diana Matar, Josh Peterson, Leigh Saffold, Annie Wells, and Julie Winokur. I am also especially grateful to my photography students who helped edit the photographs: David Drabkin, Derek Metzger, Abe Nachbaur, and Brenna Sulat.

I owe endless gratitude to my amazing editor, Natalie Kaire, for her patience and professionalism, and to everyone at Hyperion for their hard work. I am eternally indebted to my agent, Laurie Fox, for her unwavering support—and for suggesting the idea in the first place. Thanks to everyone at the Linda Chester Literary Agency for all they have done on my behalf.

Finally, I owe immense gratitude to my beloved husband, Russell Vernick, who has inspired my passionate interest in the meaning of marriage. I thank him for loving me, supporting me, and spending the most ordinary yet remarkable ten minutes with me at the end of each day.